WHeN GRaNNY WON oLYMPic GoLD

aND oTHeR MeDaL-WiNNiNG PoeMs

First published 2012 by
A & C Black
Bloomsbury Publishing plc
50 Bedford Square
London WC1B 3DP

www.acblack.com

Collection copyright © 2012 Graham Denton

The rights of Graham Denton to be identified
as the editor of this work has been asserted by him
in accordance with the Copyrights, Designs and Patents Act 1988.

ISBN 978-1-4081-3149-7

A CIP catalogue for this book is available from the British Library.

This book is produced using paper that is made from wood
grown in managed, sustainable forests. It is natural, renewable
and recyclable. The logging and manufacturing processes conform
to the environmental regulations of the country of origin.

Printed and bound by CPI Group (UK) Ltd, Croydon, CR0 4YY

3 5 7 9 10 8 6 4

WHEN GRANNY WON
OLYMPIC GOLD

AND OTHER
MEDAL-WINNING
POEMS

Chosen by **Graham Denton**

A & C Black • London

CONTENTS

SPORTY FAMILY

IF THESE WERE OLYMPIC SPORTS...

THE STRONGEST TEAM

AniMaLYMpics!

oH No!

WHO WANTS TO Be AN oLYMpic MeDALLiST?

UNBeLievABLe SPORTS FACTS!

WORDs iN THe WiND

SPORTY FAMiLY

WHEN GRANNY WON OLYMPIC GOLD

The runners took their starting blocks.
Their eyes were bright and bold,
while, from the stands, the people watched
to see who'd win the gold.

Then, all at once, they turned and stared,
and silence filled the stands
as Granny walked across the field,
a basket in her hands.

She spread a blanket on the ground
and sweetly gave a smile;
then called out to the runners,
"Sit with Granny for a while.

"I've got a lovely picnic here
with sandwiches and cake.
You've all been playing much too hard.
I'm sure you need a break."

The runners shrugged and gave a sigh
then sat down one by one.
To disappoint a Granny, well,
that simply wasn't done.

She served them ham and cheese on rye
and plates of deviled eggs.
"Now just you sit and eat," she said,
"while I go stretch my legs."

Then, glad to give them each a chance
to rest and eat and talk,
Granny and her orthopedic sneakers
took a walk.

And, as the judges scratched their heads,
around the track she strolled.
And that's how, fourteen minutes later,
Granny won the gold.

So if you are a runner,
here's advice you ought to take:
you'd best beware the basket
of a Granny who can bake.

Eric Ode

MY GRAMP

My Gramp has got a medal.
On the front there is a runner.
On the back it says:
Senior Boys 100 yards
First William Green.
I asked him about it, but before he could reply
Gran said, "Don't listen to his tales.
The only running he did was after the girls."
Gramp gave a chuckle
and went out the back
to get the tea.
As he shuffled down the passage
with his back bent,
I tried to imagine him,
legs flying, chest out,
breasting the tape.
But I couldn't.

John Foster

SPORTY FAMILY

Dad's always wrestling (with the crossword);
Granny's brilliant at running (the bath);
Mum's good at curling (her hair);
Grandad loves bowls (of ice cream);
My brother's great at diving (into bed);
My sisters are experts at rowing (with each other);
And I'm very keen on polo (mints).
What a sporty family! (not).

Andy Seed

TALKING FOR ENGLAND

Mum says my Aunty Dot could talk for England.
Could somebody else's Aunty speak for Spain
                              chin-wag for China
                              prattle for Poland
                              natter for Norway
                              jaw for Japan
                              rabbit on for Russia
                              or gossip for Greece?
And with all that noise how would we hear who'd won?

Sue Cowling

A LIKING FOR STRIKING

We are a boxing family—
My dad, my mum, my sis, and me...

My dad's a super heavyweight
A hulky, bulky fighter
My mum's a bruising cruiserweight
(though only that bit lighter)
My sis, a belting welterweight,
Could give you quite a lickin'
And me? Well, I'm a featherweight
'Cause I am just a chicken!

Graham Denton

TOO YOUNG

My dad says I'm still a little too small
To compete in the London 2012s.
So, at the age of eight,
I've decided to wait
And keep my dreams on the shelves.

In another four years (or maybe four more)
Is the date I'm now planning to go—
And each time we have tea
Dad announces to me:
"On your marks, Mark, get set, grow!"

Mike Barfield

BROTHERS

Big
Strong
Billy
Matthews
Is
Very
Very
Tall,
Which
Makes
Him
Perfectly
Suited
For
Playing   Though his brother who is short
Basketball.   Is also good at sport.

Peter Cole

SoMe oF MY SPORTY MATeS*

Snooker-table Mabel
Go go-kartin' Martin
Swiss mountain ski Marie
Motorbikey Mikey
Skateboard dude Mamood

Muscle-toner Mona
Cricket-batty Matty
Great-goal-scorin' Maureen
Ride-a-filly Millie
Sprint-like-crazy Maisie...

...and a marathon racer called
I-can-run-for Miles.

Nick Toczek

* My sporty mates all have names beginning with M. Can you think up some beginning with other letters?

IF THESE WERE
OLYMPIC SPORTS...

I WOULD WIN THE GOLD IF THESE WERE OLYMPIC SPORTS...

Bubble gum blowing
Goggle box watching
Late morning snoring
Homework botching

Quilt ruffling
Little brother teasing
Pizza demolishing
Big toe cheesing

Insult hurling, wobbly throwing
Infinite blue belly button fluff growing

Late-night endurance computer screen gazing
Non-attentive open-jawed eyeball glazing

Ultimate volume decibel blaring
Long-distance marathon same sock wearing

Recognize all these as sports then meet
Me! The Champ Apathetic Athlete!

Paul Cookson

SLEEP ON IT

I dreamed last night
That pillow-fighting
Had been made
An Olympic sport.

Unlike the boxing,
There was only
One category—
Featherweight.

Mike Barfield

GOLD MEDAL KID

Two million eyes are watching me;
a million tongues are cheering.
The fears I might have felt before
are quickly disappearing.

Tonight I'm feeling ready—
completely on my game.
My nerves are cool as arctic ice.
I'm hotter than a flame.

I turn and twist, and float and fly,
as if my arms were wings.
I rise so high I touch the sky—
my legs are filled with springs.

I scoff and laugh at gravity,
defying all its laws.
With every leap, I hear the cheers,
and thunderous applause.

Olympic dreams of glory
are soaring in my head.
For I'm the best who ever lived
at bouncing on my bed.

Ted Scheu

NON-OLYMPIC SPORTS I'M GOOD AT

Peach volleyball
Mountain baking
Chocolate kayak
Marathon (eating)
Orange squash
Platelifting
The 100 litres (of Coke)
Ice cream hockey
Pieathlon

Andy Seed

ye olDe SPORTes

There were sports that were played
A long time ago.
Some you'll have heard of
But some you won't know.

Fighting with dragons
And burning of witches
(And football was played
Long before they had pitches).

Bull baiting, cock fighting,
Prize fighting, too,
And wrestling with wild boars
In tubs of cold stew.

Tossing the cayman,
Throwing the shark,
And blindfolded archery
(Played after dark).

Catching the javelin
And heading the shot...
They're no longer played.
I wonder why not?

Ian Larmont

RECORDS I HOLD
(IN OUR HOUSE)

Tallest structure built with toast (63cms)
Highest number of trampoline bounces on the bed (137)
Most sultanas pushed up nose (74)
Largest number of snails balanced on head (11)
Shortest time in the shower (9 seconds)
Longest time hiding from my sister in a box (half an hour)
Shortest time to eat an ice-cream (1 minute and a bit)
Longest time wearing the same pair of socks (three weeks)

Roger Stevens

SPORTS

Playing tennis,
I'm no menace.
As for croquet,
I'm just "OK".

Then there's cricket—
Can't quite lick it.
Ditto: rowing,
Discus-throwing.

Also: biking,
Jogging, hiking,
Ten-pin bowling,
And pot-holing.

Can't play hockey.
I'm no jockey,
Daren't go riding,
Or hang-gliding.

Nor can I jump
Long or high jump.
Being sporty
Ain't my *forté*.

I'm pathetic,
Unathletic,
But at dinner...
I'm a winner!

Colin West

VIRTUALLY A LEGEND

I triumphed in the PGA,
Nick Faldo blew his chance.
Top scorer in the NBA.
I've raced la Tour de France.
I would have won the FA Cup
but Mum said, "Time for tea!
Come on, son, you've had enough,
so please turn off the Wii!"

Paul Hughes

THE STRONGEST TEAM

HOW I BECAMe A
BLACK BeLT

A week ago Sunday with weather so warm,
karate class met in the park.
We practiced our kicks, then we studied our form
and chopped at the sycamore bark.

I sat and I rested beneath that great tree
while Christopher worked on his stance.
My mind was so focused that I didn't see
the ants marching straight up my pants.

The ants in my britches were biting me there.
The bite marks were starting to swell.
I itched, so I kicked and I clawed at the air,
then spun as I let out a yell.

I twirled and I jumped with such dizzying speed
while trying to scratch at the bites.
The teachers looked on and then quickly agreed
my skills had reached masterful heights.

For twenty-three minutes I pranced without pause.
I shrieked at each itchy red welt.
I finished at last to the master's applause.
He bowed and he gave me his belt.

Jeff Mondak

RUDO

Jude's judo was extremely rude
'Cause Jude did judo in the nude.
And all the judo judges felt
He should at least have worn his belt.

Mike Barfield

BeLieve it oR Knot

My brother's on the wrestling team—
   I like to watch him wrestle,
And see him get all tangled up
   And shaped just like a pretzel.

With one leg over, one arm through—
   All twisted 'round in spots,
I find it is the coolest way
   To learn my Boy Scout knots!

Robert Scotellaro

MiLO OF CROTON: 540 B.C.E.

When young Milo the Wrestler would fight,
no opponent could outmatch his might.
In a time before Zero
this Greek superhero
was a star of Olympian height.

Adding weight to his frame and his fame,
he ate meat before every Big Game.
One legend tells how
he devoured a whole cow!
Is that bull? That's what some scholars claim.

To perform for the Greek multitude,
all the wrestlers would fight in the nude.
Well-oiled, they were dressed
in their birthday-suit best
and nobody viewed it as rude.

Milo's name has lived on through the years.
In great stories and art he appears.
Marble statues survive—
he looks almost alive
wrestling still, to the spectators' cheers.

Avis Harley

SUMO WRESTLERS

Sumo wrestlers
Grab folds of flesh
Pink as old pyjamas,
And heave and grunt
On the soft, white square
Of their playpen.

And when they hitch up
Their huge nappies,
And when their squashy faces
Crumple with pain,
They seem to me
Like the lost babies
Of beanstalk giants.

Clare Bevan

THE BEAST

Inside a wire cage,
The hammer-thrower stands;
Outsider of the games,
Wild beast of the land.

His shoulders arch and tense,
He snorts, his nostrils flare,
He focuses his eyes
With a concentrated stare.

Then round and round he goes,
The wire taut and strong,
The handle is released,
His throw is smooth and long.

The crowd erupt and cheer,
Amazed by the composure
Of this beastly athlete,
Kept in an enclosure.

Coral Rumble

PUTTING THE SHOT

Tomorrow I may put the shot,
Or on the other hand, may not;
For yesterday I put the shot,
But where I put it, I forgot.

Colin West

THE RUGBY TOURNAMENT

At the end of the last match of the season
there were four front teeth

poking out of the pitch,
two players had one arm each in a sling,

and there were possibly three little toes broken—
all on left feet.

Five sets of parents were hoarse from shouting
and couldn't go to work the next day.

Seven grans had hypothermia,
despite being wrapped in twelve tartan rugs.

Three little sisters have very snotty colds.
Everybody is dying for the next season to begin.

Chrissie Gittins

FLYNN'S FIST

Cried the fist of a boxer named Flynn,
"Sore and bruised is the state I am in.
If it's not someone's nose
That's delivering blows
Then I'm pounded by somebody's chin!"

Philip Waddell

STRONGEST TEAM

We're the strongest team in town,
as other teams can tell.
We haven't got the strongest arms—
we've got the strongest smell.

Ted Scheu

AniMALYMPics!

WHENEVER YAKS PLAY BASKETBALL

Whenever yaks play basketball
it isn't any fun at all.
Their games are always such a snore.
They never shoot. They never score.

It seems they don't enjoy the sport.
They never run around the court.
Instead they simply settle back
and yak, and yak, and yak, and yak.

Kenn Nesbitt

A RaBBiT RaCeD a TuRTLe...

A rabbit raced a turtle.
You know the turtle won.
And Mr Rabbit came in late,
a very hot cross bun!

Anon

THe ARk oLYMpicS

Well, after thirty days afloat,
The animals grew bored—
The Ark just bobbed about all day
While creatures snoozed. And snored.
"We need a little something
To amuse us," someone roared.

But Noah, being clever,
Was ahead of them, and so
He launched the Ark Olympics
With a mighty whistle-blow,
While Mrs Noah flapped the flag
And shouted: "Off you go!"

The first race was the Marathon
Around and round the deck—
A wrinkled rhino took the lead
Although he looked a wreck,
But then a small giraffe whizzed by
And beat him by a neck.

The next event was 'High Jump'
Which was fun for frogs and fleas
And also bouncy kangaroos
Who won their heat with ease,
While both the desert camels
Grabbed the gold for 'Knobbly Knees'.

'Hide-and-Seek' was battled out
By squirrels, mice and moles,
(Who like to squirm down tunnels
Or to bury stuff in holes).
The woodlice were delighted
With their prize for 'Forward Rolls'.

The spiders won the 'Bungee Drop'
With style and speed, of course.
The 'Tail Swishing' medal went
To Dobbin (Noah's horse).
A MOST annoying parrot won
'Sweet Singing'. What a sauce!

The zebras and the tigers shared
The prize for 'Posh Pyjamas'.
Two snakes inside a basket swiped
'The World's Most Slinky Charmers',
And (yuck!) 'Long-Distance Spitting'
Was a triumph for the llamas.

The elephants, I'm glad to say,
Were best at 'Lifting Weights'.
ALL the monkeys earned gold stars
For 'Juggling With Plates',
An octopus (just visiting)
Won 'Adding Up In Eights'.

By supper time, the animals
Were ready for their beds.
They snuggled in their nests and nooks
And leaky wooden sheds,
As Mr Noah winked his eye
And: "Well done ME," he said.

Clare Bevan

SiLk Tie

Two silk worms had a race.
But neither won the chase.
And here's the reason why:
They ended in a tie.

Graham Denton

THE FiSHLYMpics

The Olympics of Fish kicked off after dawn,
The coral reef hurdles were won by a prawn.
Best Synchronised Swimming was claimed by the cod,
Which really annoyed the whole tuna fish squad.

A shoal scored a goal, then a sole threw a pole,
A squid grabbed a scallop and started to bowl.
The seals clapped and barked, and they did it so well,
That a young hermit crab did a streak with no shell.

A swordfish won fencing with one mighty swish,
The high jump was made by a high flying fish.
Both boxing and dancing were won by a lobster,
Which upset the bookie—a manta ray mobster.

A footballing haddock caused havoc with skill,
He weaved past defenders (two sharks and a krill).
But an octopus made a spectacular save,
And all of the fish did a Mexican wave.

Nick Murphy

THeRe WAS A YOUNG LADY OF VeNice

There was a young lady of Venice
Who used hard-boiled eggs to play tennis.
When they said, "It seems wrong,"
She remarked, "Go along!
You don't know how prolific my hen is!"

Anon

THe LiTTLe oLYMPics

When fleas bite your ankles
Their leaping skill rankles
Despite all their neat somersaulting;
But when you've a fleabite
At neck, chest or knee height,
It means that the beasts are pole-vaulting.

Nick Toczek

SPORTS DOG

They say that I'm a 'sports dog'—
But I'm still just a pup,
And I don't know what sport I ought
To do when I grow up.

Yes, I'm meant to be a sports dog—
My owners both say so;
But just what sort of sport I ought
To do, I just don't know.

Perhaps I'll be a footballer,
Who dribbles, shoots and scores—
But suppose they call it handball
Just for using my front paws?

Perhaps I'll drive in races
To win trophies, cups and medals—
But *how* can I drive cars at all?
My paws can't reach the pedals.

Perhaps I'll be a pole-vaulter—
Is *that* my sporting role?
But with my paws I'd find it hard
To even hold the pole.

Hurraff!* At last I understand
What all this 'sports dog' talk is!
My sport's not football, racing cars,
Or pole-vaulting. It's walkies!

David Bateman

* 'Hurraff!' is dog-language for 'Hurray!'

AcRostic

Right feet wedged against the blocks,
Eager limbs met focussed brains.
Athletes faced their foes, the clock,
Deafened by the crowd's acclaim.
Young, we hoped to prove our strength,

Smashing records, seeking fame.
Each would go to any length,
Thrusting forth to stake our claim.

"GO!" cried Miss. I ran, but soon,
Off it fell. My egg! Damn spoon!

Paul Hughes

OH NO!

Oh no,
The race
Has been
Cancelled—

Just before
Their main course
Someone ate
The starter.

Andy Seed

HOLiDAY PRiNT

There was a young man from Dundee
Who had a great passion to ski,
He skied with aggression,
And left an impression—
The shape of himself on a tree!

Coral Rumble

SPLASHPOINT

I'm inclined to believe a
Diving 'Diva'
Might have won the gold medal, except
With water, the pool
Was only half-full—
As she found out soon after she leapt...!

Trevor Harvey

SHORT STORY

Little Willie;
Pair of skates;
Hole in ice;
Pearly Gates!

Anon

R.I.P.

The javelin
was travellin';
The judge
didn't budge.

Graham Denton

A DARiNG YOUNG GYMNAST

A daring young gymnast called Fritz
did, as his finale, the splits.
It raised quite a laugh
when he split right in half
and was carried away in two bits.

Marian Swinger

WRONG JUMP

I ran, leapt, swung up high,
over the heads of passers-by,
over the traffic, the lampposts, the wires,
the rooftops, the chimneys, the towers and spires,
The House of Lords, of Commons, Big Ben,
the top of the London Eye, and then—

down I tumbled, bump-bump-bump,
to the gloomy boom of the judge: "No jump!"

"But why?" I cried. "I jumped to the sky!"
"Wrong jump," he sighed. "This is *long*, not *high*."

Kate Williams

WHO WANTS TO BE AN OLYMPIC MEDALLIST?

WHO WANTS TO BE AN OLYMPIC MEDALLIST?

Well, I certainly don't!

All that training?
Two, three, four times a day?
I couldn't stand it.
I'm far too busy
Texting my mates,
Trimming my toenails,
Bathing the gerbil,
Eating pink marshmallows,
Making paper elephants,
Counting my shoes,
Walking the dog,
Practising the tuba,
Growing my hair,
Measuring string,
Telling tall stories,
Staring at the rain.

But then again,
I could see myself,
The gold heavy round my neck,
Bursting with pride
As the anthem plays...

An Olympic medallist?

Maybe I should give it a go?

H. A. Fairlie

Recipe for an Olympic Athlete

Take one portion of Natural Talent.
Add a large dollop of Determination. Mix together well.
Stir in 1 or 2 Sacrifices to strengthen the resolve.
Combine with hours of high quality Training (the vigorous type). Repeat this daily for several years.
Carefully add Focus then sprinkle generously with the Desire to Win.
Finally, place under the spotlight and add pressure to perform.
Will now be ready to serve at all major competitions.

Jane Saddler

ATHLETE ZEAL

Athletes
Brilliantly
Compete
During
Earth's
Foremost
Games.

High-powered
Individuals
Justify
Kudos—
Launching
Magnificent,
Nail-biting
Olympics.
Pulses
Quicken...

Record-breakers
Seek
The
Ultimate
Victory
With
X-uberant
Youthful
Zeal.

Avis Harley

I COULD, YOU KNOW...

I could hurdle the hurdliest hurdles in the world
I could curl the coolest curling stone ever curled
I could jump the trickiest triple jump ever jumped
I could stump the wickedest cricket wicket ever
stumped
I could sock the hockiest hockey ball ever socked
I could lock the lockiest head-lock ever locked
I could throw the showiest judo throw ever thrown
I could row the rowiest single scull ever rown
I could snatch the weightiest weightlift ever snatched
I could catch the bounciest rounder ever catched
I could serve the swerviest first serve ever served
I could curve the curviest curve ball ever curved
I could slamdunk the dinkiest basket ever dunked
I could trunk the swishiest swimming stroke ever
trunked
I could dive the swallowest swallow dive ever dived
I could five the most modern Modern Pentathlon
ever fived
I could put the hottest shotput ever putted
I could foot the finest football ever footed
I could ace the bestest baseball ever aced
I could pace the raciest road race ever paced
I could pole the most faultless vaulting ever poled
I could hole the holiest golf putt ever holed
I could toss the sharpest javelin ever tossed
I could cross the crossest cross-country ever crossed

In fact, I could easily be king of the ring, rule the pool, take the lake, bewitch the pitch, force the course, seize the seas, eat the street, steal the field, AND be the championest Champion of Champions trackside...
If only, maybe, one day soon, I got up off my backside.

Mike Barfield

TRAINING

No-one else is up yet,
Every house is dark,
No-one else is up yet,
I hear a vixen bark.

No-one else is up yet
As I start to run,
No-one else is up yet,
Except the waking sun.

No-one else is up yet,
Up over the big-H stile,
No-one else is up yet,
Every yard seems like a mile.

No-one else is up yet,
Run under winter trees,
No-one else is up yet,
Feel sweat-sharp edge and freeze.

No-one else is up yet,
Skim frost-whiskered grass,
No-one else is up yet,
Look up, the sky's stained glass.

No-one else is up yet
But now I'm a thawed-out stream,
No-one else is up yet,
It's like flying in a dream.

No-one else is up yet,
And I'll keep on keeping on,
No-one else is up yet,
Until I reach the horizon.

Kevin McCann

SpeeD

Jeffery won the hundred metres
At the annual High School sports.
Was it the diet and training that did it?
Or was it the wasp down his shorts?

Granville Lawson

I AM HUFFING, I AM PUFFING

I am huffing, I am puffing,
I can barely catch my breath,
I feel perilously perched upon
the verge of certain death,
I am absolutely shattered,
I am positively bushed,
I have pushed myself much further
than a human should be pushed.

I feel fit for next to nothing,
I am almost on the deck,
I'm devoid of any vigour,
I am virtually a wreck,
all my muscles are complaining,
and my legs are lumps of lead,
there's a knot inside my stomach,
I've an aching in my head.

I can hardly move an eyelid,
I've got nothing left to give,
I have reached the utter limits,
I have lost my will to live,
this is when the coach announces
—as he primes his starting gun—
"Right you lot, the warm-up's over...
now it's time to start your run!"

Graham Denton

uNBeLievaBLe SPORTS FACTS!

UNBELIEVABLE SPORTS FACTS!

Tennis one more than nine.
Badminton is an evil form of goodminton.
If you go round a track twice on a bike you're recycling.
Grasshoppers like cricket.
When wildebeest paddle small boats they're gnuing.
Hearse racing is dead good.
Last year they compared all the motorsports and Formula won.
Crossing the Atlantic on a 747 is not plane sailing.
A donkey once appeared at the Badminton Horse Trials—it was found guilty.
Unbelievable!

Andy Seed

FReD LORZ - THE MARATHON CHEAT 1904

Fred Lorz
Completed the Marathon course
Way ahead of the field.

Later his secret was revealed.
It wasn't that his running had been so swift...
He'd stopped a car and taken a lift.

John Coldwell

A JAVELIN THROWER CALLED VICKY

A javelin thrower called Vicky
found the grip of her javelin sticky.
When it came to the throw
she just couldn't let go—
making judging the distance quite tricky.

Anon

BATTY SPORTS BOOKS TOP TEN BESTSELLERS (AS COMPILED BY ARTHUR LETICS)

Learning To Shot Put by Eva Brick
Weight Lifting Disasters by Buster Gutt
Elastic Gymnastics by Horace Zontalbars
Horsing Around by Jim Carner
The Art of Pace-making by Justin Front
Fair-Weather Fans by Wendy Rainstops
Winning Out Of Sight by I. Malone
Running The Marathon by Percy Verence
The 100 Yard Dash by Willie Makit
You'll Never Catch Me by Hedda De Field

Graham Denton

STROKE OF LUCK

"Why are you wearing two pairs of pants?"
Asked the golfer's son.
"Well, my lad,"
Replied his dad,
"I might get a hole in one."

Peter Cole

TUG O'WAR

Years ago, I met a man
Who told me he was
An official referee
At tug o'war contests.

He said that
Tug o'war was one
Of the few sports
Which you win by
Going backwards.

He was right, but
I actually knew that fact already.
(Rowing is another,
In case you were wondering.)

However, he also told me
That the people on a
Tug o'war team
Don't pull or tug on the rope.
Real tug o'war contestants
Say they 'push' rope.

Well, at the time, I believed him.
But now I'm not so sure.
Perhaps he was just
Pushing my leg.

Mike Barfield

DLOG ROF GNIWOR

FOR SiR STeveN ReDGRAve

gnisirprus ehT
gniwor tuoba gniht
ecar uoy :si
gnikool tuohtiw
!gniog er'uoy erehw

Mike Johnson

THE LIGHT AT THE END

The fastest 1500-meter run
By someone with a disability—
Noel Thatcher (1991)—
A lesson in daring, humility,
The will power of humankind.

He was blind.

J. Patrick Lewis

[Note: Noel Thatcher of Great Britain won
the 1,500 m race in 3:55:00, Leeds, England, 1991.
Cf. *The Guinness Book of Records*, 1999, p, 465.]

FiRsT SeRvice

Here's a fact you might not know—
Tennis is the oldest sport.
How exactly is that so?
Moses served in Pharaoh's court!

Graham Denton

THe LORD SAiD UNTO MOSeS

The Lord said unto Moses:
"Come forth."
But he slipped on a banana skin
And came fifth.

Anon

SOFTBALL?

They call it
a *soft*ball,
but how
can that be?

My head just met
that *soft*ball
and it
does not agree.

Ted Scheu

WORDs iN
THE WiND

WORDS IN THE WIND

When bike riders are out on a race
being mindful of keeping the pace,
then perhaps they might miss
a remark such as this
when the wind and the wheels interlace...

Whispers wind to bike's thin spinning wheels:
"You are kinder than automobiles.
When you comb through my air
and you part with such care,
how delicious your bi-tickle feels!"

Avis Harley

WEIGHTLIFTER

He rubs his hands with powder
and it puffs into the air like pollen.
He squares up to the earth
presses his feet into the floor
like a rooting tree.
He thinks.
Pushes all the power
of his mind into his muscles.
Braces his bones.

Then
bend
snatch
lift
dragon-roar breath
fire in the blood.

He stands – an X –
and offers slabs of iron
held high like sacrificial meat
to a savage hungry god.

Jan Dean

SoMe RiDDLes TO THROW YOU!

1.
Graceful airborne spear,
soaring, dipping, swallow-like—
Earth welcomes you home.

2.
Human cannon fire:
muscled limbs launch steel boulders
that dent the earth's crust.

3.
The whirl of an arm:
metal plate walking on air;
white line voyager.

4.
Bodies spin like tops,
sending long-tailed birds of iron
on freedom's brief flight.

Ian Brown

1. Javelin 2. Shot put 3. Discus 4. Hammer

CiNQUAiN

Twisting
on the High Bar
with dizzying swiftness
this aerodynamic spit-roast
sizzles.

Graham Denton

HAIKU

Clearing the bar, she
    falls through silence and into
        all that unleashed breath.

Kevin McCann

THe WiNNiNG Dive

on the high board, I walk above the water. And

t
e
e
f

e
r
a
B
                    D

                          I

                             V

                               E

                 A perfect
entry – almost no splash at
all. The rushing in my ears
hushes the sound of the
crowd. In the cool blue the
water whispers my name.

H. A. Fairlie

86

SWiMMiNG

The water strokes my body
as if I were its pet.
I'm slipping through its fingers:
they really don't feel wet.
We're travelling together
but haven't got there yet.
It's gentle, friendly, playful.
I'm very glad we met.

Jill Townsend

SLALOM

Swift
          crisp
angl-
          ing
black
          ant
   on
          dazz-
   ling
          snow
crys-
          tals
   gra-
          zing
   blue
          red
gates
          swish

swish-
   ing
fast-
   er
ev-
   er
fast-
   er
  to
   t
finish line
  e

Rosemary Hodi

TWENTY-SIX MILES

Marathon man, why do you run
Twenty-six miles into the sun?

> The fire and the heat and the body beating
> Rhythms speeding to the town below.

Marathon woman, how can you stand
Twenty-six miles of white beach sand?

> The wind and the waves and the heart repeating
> Wordsongs whispered so long ago.

J. Patrick Lewis

THE CLOSING CEREMONY

On the last day of the Games
The athletes mingle and weave
Like colourful threads in a tapestry of stars.

The Fastest Sprinter In All The World
Looks at a wiry marathon-runner
And says to himself:
"Of course I can race in swift circles,
But she can battle with boredom and pain
For mile after pitiless mile.
How wonderful she is."

The Wiry Marathon-Runner
Gazes at a tall javelin-thrower
And says to herself:
"Of course I have patience and pace,
But he can slice the summer air
With his sudden, shimmering spears.
How astonishing he is."

The Tall Javelin-Thrower
Shakes hands with a tiny gymnast
And says to himself:
"Of course my powers impress the crowd,
But she can cast a spell of silence
When she spins above the perilous beam.
How fearless she is."

The Tiny Gymnast
Waves at a huge weightlifter
And says to herself:
"Of course I can curve my flexible spine,
But he can mock the gods of gravity
With his mighty grip, his shining shoulders.
How magnificent he is."

The Huge Weightlifter
Nods at a beautiful pentathlon winner
And says to himself:
"Of course I could lift her with one hand,
But she can juggle with five slippery skills
Without ever losing her smile.
How versatile she is."

The Beautiful Pentathlon Winner
Glances at a shy sportsman
And says to herself:
"Of course I have learned a handful of tricks,
But he is quite simply,
Quite splendidly,
The Fastest Sprinter In All The World.
How modest he is."

The Child In The Crowd
Cheers and shouts to anyone who cares to listen:
"How speedy, how strong, how brave,
How brilliant they all are."
But no one hears him.

The fireworks have begun.

Clare Bevan

ACKNOWLEDGEMENTS

All poems are copyright © the authors and have been included by kind permission of the copyright holders. Grateful acknowledgement is made to the publishers of the following publications in which poems previously appeared.

All efforts have been made to seek permission for copyright material, but in the event of omissions, the publisher would be pleased to hear from the copyright holders and to amend these acknowledgements in subsequent editions

Not to be reproduced without permission.

'The Beast' copyright © Coral Rumble 2010.

'Brothers' by Peter Cole first published in *Michael Rosen's A-Z: The Best Children's Poetry from Agard to Zephaniah*, Puffin, 2009.

'A Daring Young Gymnast' by Marian Swinger first published in *Loopy Limericks*, Collins, 2001.

'Flynn's Fist' by permission of Philip Waddell.

'Gold Medal Kid' by Ted Scheu, first appeared in *I Threw My Brother Out: A Laughable Line up of Sports Poems* by Ted Scheu (Young Poets Press, 2010) 'Haiku' by permission of Kevin McCann.

'Holiday Print' first published in *Breaking the Rules*, Coral Rumble, Lion Hudson 2004.

'How I Became A Black Belt' by Jeff Mandak-first appeared in *I Hope I Don't Strike Out* created by Bruce Lansky (Meadowbrook Press, 2008).

'The Little Olympics' by Nick Toczek previously appeared in Nick Toczek's collection *Hogs'n'Dogs'n'Slugs'n'Bugs* (Caboodle Books 2008) subsequently republished as *Cats'n'Bats'n'Slugs'n'Bugs* (Caboodle Books 2009).

'I Would Win The Gold If These Were Olympic Sports...' by Paul Cookson, first appeared in *Crazy Classrooms and Secret Staffrooms* by Paul Cookson (Lion Hudson, 2001).

'My Gramp' by John Foster copyright © John Foster 2007 from *The Poetry Chest* (Oxford University Press), included by permission of the author.

'Putting the Shot' copyright © Colin West. Reprinted by permission.

'The Rugby Tournament' by Chrissie Gittins first appeared in *Now You See Me, Now You...* (Rabbit Hole Publications).

'Speed' by Granville Lawson first appeared in *I Say, I Say, I Say and Other Joke Poems* compiled by John Foster (Oxford University Press, 2003).

'Sports' © Colin West. Reprinted by permission.

'Sports Dog' copyright © David Bateman.

'Strongest Team' by Ted Scheu previously appeared in the anthology *Miles of Smiles*, 2004, Meadowbrook Press, USA.

'Sumo Wrestlers' by Clare Bevan first published in *The Cowpat-Throwing Contest* edited by Brian Moses, Hodder Wayland 2000.

'Swimming' copyright © Jill Townsend 2011.

'Talking for England' by permission of Sue Cowling.

'Training' by permission of Kevin McCann.

'Whenever Yaks Play Basketball' by Kenn Nesbitt first appeared in *The Tighty Whitey Spider: And More Wacky Animal Poems I Totally Made Up* by Kenn Nesbitt (Sourcebooks, 2010).